BBC MUSIC GUIDES

SCHUBERT SONGS

BBC MUSIC GUIDES

BBC MUSIC GUIDES

SCHUBERT SONGS

BY

MAURICE J. E. BROWN

BRITISH BROADCASTING CORPORATION

Published by the British Broadcasting Corporation
35 Marylebone High Street, London W.1

ISBN: 0 563 07302 0

First published 1967

Reprinted 1972, 1975, 1977, 1982

Printed in Great Britain by
Spottiswoode Ballantyne Ltd., Colchester and London

CONTENTS

I

THE YOUNG SCHUBERT

A glance through the early pages of O. E. Deutsch's *Thematic Catalogue* of Schubert's works[1] shows that the composer, in his schooldays, was not particularly drawn to the writing of songs as a musical experience. His youthful devotion was to established musical forms and structures such as the sonata, string quartet, symphony, opera, and Mass. In the course of his deliberate essays in all these familiar forms, each one hallowed by many years of honour and acclaim, each one adorned by masterpieces from the pens of his musical gods, Schubert encountered the song as a humble member of the varied assemblage even though, as is often the case with humble members of a community, the spawning was prolific. We can imagine how, as Schubert explored this lowly department of music-making, the attraction of setting poetry to the melodies which rose so easily in his mind became stronger and the experience more satisfying. When, in October 1814, he completed 'Gretchen am Spinnrade', there was no longer any question of being 'particularly drawn' to the writing of songs: he was a dedicated youth, and his destiny had claimed him.

The more one studies the enormous field of pre-Schubertian song, the more apparent it becomes that any historical – in the sense of evolutionary – approach is impossible. The Schubert songs from 1814 to 1828 are not the crowning stage in a slowly growing edifice of development: they are merely further pages in a long catalogue of entries. It is misleading to point to a few firm and attractive songs composed by Haydn, Mozart and Beethoven, which is all that most of us know of the pre-Schubertian *Lied*, and then to name the early masterpieces of Schubert, as if that told the whole story – as if the four composers had consciously striven towards a creation of the *Lied*. These isolated songs, Haydn's 'She never told her love' (*Twelfth Night*) or 'The Spirit's Song', Mozart's 'Das Veilchen' or 'Abendempfindung' and Beethoven's *An die ferne Geliebte* song-cycle, have little in common with each other and do nothing to suggest an evolving song-form. Nor did they affect the work of established song writers of that time, men such as J. A. Schulz, J. A. Hiller, J. R.

[1] London, 1951.

Zumsteeg, J. K. Reichardt and C. F. Zelter. And it is the songs of these minor figures, not those of Haydn, Mozart and Beethoven, which were Schubert's models; we have documentary evidence for this, as well as the evidence of his own juvenile efforts. Nor can we doubt that he knew well the work of an active group of Viennese song composers whose names have scant memorials in the music encyclopedias, but whose prolific output between 1770 and 1800 cannot possibly have been unknown to any musician in Vienna of that day: Josef Anton Steffan, Carl Friberth, Johann Holzer, and many others. These men composed music to lyrics which have become famous in non-German-speaking lands by reason of Schubert's treatment of them later on: poems by Klopstock, Matthisson, Hölty, as well as by Goethe and Schiller. The songs of these Viennese composers, moreover, have a certain tunefulness characteristic of South Germany and Austria, which is not present to the same degree in the songs of their more famous counterparts in North Germany. In this way they prepare us a little for the advent of Schubert's melodic richness. The North German composers introduced the dramatic (in the sense of histrionic) and serious elements of the *Lied*, which, particularly in Zumsteeg, were to impress the young Schubert deeply. Their songs grew from a more sophisticated treatment of folk-song, with infiltrations from the operatic world, and a growing realization that the finer the poetry chosen for their songs, the more fruitful the musical possibilities which the text evoked; Schulz, we know, like Wolf later on, insisted on poetic worth in his song-texts. As for Beethoven's songs, by the time his song-cycle *An die ferne Geliebte* was published in 1817, Schubert had forged the modern *Lied*, and was by then far beyond the reach of any past or contemporary song-composer.

The earliest extant Schubert song is 'Hagars Klage' (30 March 1811), but it is not his first effort in this sphere as his brother Ferdinand and his school friends have told us. Even before he tried his hand at song-writing we can imagine him subconsciously absorbing the possibilities of the solo song as it existed in the early years of the nineteenth century. It is necessary to consider those possibilities if we are to appreciate the less immediately obvious qualities of his songs and to realize fully his total response to the poem he set. It would be tedious to enumerate all the features which Schubert found in the song-books of his

7

immediate predecessors, tedious and unnecessary, for some of these features – the prolonged instrumental prelude, for instance – fell, so far as Schubert was concerned, on stony ground. Others bore fruit, and it is the germinating elements in the work of Zumsteeg and his fellow song-writers that can profitably be looked at.

There is, first, the treatment of the poet's introductory, or interpolated, question whereby the words are set to a declamatory or recitative phrase; Schubert learnt from these song-writers how arrestingly a song could be introduced in this way, or how effectively the flow of the music could be interrupted and then resumed with fresh interest when the poet's thought is deliberately broken by a direct or implied question and the music similarly breaks its course. Reichardt uses the procedure in a setting of Goethe's 'Erinnerung'; here and elsewhere he actually labels these two diverse styles 'deklamiert' and 'gesungen' ('declaimed' and 'sung'). The expressive breaks in his setting of the same poet's 'Ganymed' at the words 'Wohin? ach, wohin?' are admirable. Zumsteeg in his music for Schiller's 'Die Erwartung' shows the recitative treatment of the lover's questions in a manner quite as advanced and telling as was Schubert's in his setting of the same poem. Even when Zumsteeg does not actually use the recitative, he can hold back the true lyrical start and flow of his songs by broken, parlando phrases, which hold the listener's attention by anticipation. The device in Schubert's hands leads to some of his most charming moments: that inspired treatment of the poet's question by a declamatory phrase, so welded into the musical fabric that it breaks yet still belongs – in 'Lachen und Weinen', when the girl asks why she weeps, or laughs, without reason (but her heart knows) or in 'Pause', one of Schubert's most superb uses of the device, where the young miller looks at his abandoned lute and wonders about the future.

Many of the songs of these earlier composers are greatly extended settings of long ballads. Phrases, even stanzas, are repeated over and over again in order to match the range and extent of their musical structure. Far from blaming Schubert for the repetition of the poet's words, mainly in his early songs, he deserves praise for gradually eliminating what was, in his day, an established convention, although to us an undesirable one. Yet side by side with these ample solo cantatas, there are

8

brief, epigrammatic settings of single-stanza poems – Goethe's 'Erinnerung', a four-lined verse, has been mentioned. From these short poems, Zumsteeg, Zelter and the rest produced songs of only a dozen bars in length and to this practice we owe those gems of Schubert's work in 1815 and 1816. To them, too, Schubert was indebted for the type of song conveniently labelled 'modified strophic'. The strophic song itself, in which all the verses are sung to the same music, is modified by them in conventional ways; there is little else than a change into the minor key for one or two of the stanzas, rather on the lines of the change into a minor key for one variation in a set based on a major key theme. Thus Zumsteeg, in his setting of Hölty's *Klage: An den Mond* uses an *andantino* in F major for verse 1 and a *larghetto* in F minor for verses 2 and 3. The refinement of the scheme, which Schubert's genius brought about, will be glanced at later when his setting of the same poem is considered.

When reading through the songs of four composers, Zelter, Zumsteeg, Reichardt and Konradin Kreutzer, one encounters most of the poems of Schubert's early song-settings: sufficient indication that he knew their work and was, as Spaun tells us, frankly trying to improve on it. (It is significant that none of the poems set by Mozart recurs in his work.) It is also fascinating to see how these predecessors of Schubert tackled poems such as Goethe's 'Erlkönig', 'Prometheus', 'Rastlose Liebe' or 'Ganymed', from which Schubert later forged his masterpieces. Passion, ardent declamation, variety of movement, an interesting use of the pianoforte, all these ingredients are there, only the material itself lacks a spark of the divine fire. Reichardt's 'Prometheus' and 'Rastlose Liebe' are admirable essays and if they are obvious examples of a minor composer's reach exceeding his grasp, then that is a far easier matter to forgive than the condescension of a major composer scaling down his powers to achieve a pretty song-trifle. Their settings of 'Erlkönig' cannot fail to arrest the attention of a musician who turns their pages, since he knows what Schubert will make of the poem in later years; their settings point to Loewe, of course, and not to Schubert. There is no doubt in our minds today that Goethe's ballad hardly deserves the sublimity of the music which it inspired Schubert to write. It is a ghost story, deriving ultimately from Bürger's *Lenore*: the night ride, the haunted forest, the whispering

9

ghost, the frightened child, in what way can these threadbare ingredients be considered other than that they serve well the purpose of holding 'children from play, and old men from the chimney corner'? When Zumsteeg and Reichardt start their rapid thrilling chords, one is immediately conscious of a narrator pushing his face forward, narrowing his eyes and pouting his lips, as he starts: 'Who rides so late through night and wind?' Both of them, like Loewe later on, use triple time and so preserve Goethe's partially anapaestic metre, which Schubert's 4/4 time destroys – at once elevating and redeeming the doggerel rhythm. Most of the Ossian poems which Schubert set in 1816–17 can also be found in the song-books of Zumsteeg and Zelter.

Schubert learned from these two composers how they used declamation, and devised episodic structures to suit the poet's verses; he responded to a certain throwing aside of control – a rhapsodic quality – which is present in their songs. He also learnt much from Reichardt and Kreutzer. Reichardt's songs are rhythmically very spontaneous and lively, and there is a quality of contrapuntal movement which completely frees them at times from the use of figured accompaniments. His setting of Goethe's 'Der Abschied' points to a style adopted by Schubert in many of the smaller songs of the 1820s. From Kreutzer he derived more delicate, more subtle procedures. It is necessary to remember, of course, that Kreutzer was still composing songs during the years when Schubert was at the height of his powers and, indeed, for many years after Schubert's death; we are here concerned only with those which were written before 1815, which the young Schubert would have known before his own styles were fully formed. To begin with, we find in Kreutzer's songs a sense of thematic development, which was due to the full emergence of classical sonata-form. Kreutzer composed a good deal of instrumental work in sonata-form and one is conscious of the fact in his songs. His setting of Uhland's *Heimkehr*, an *agitato* movement in D minor, is a first-rate song, and he develops theme and pianoforte figuration in a thoroughly Schubertian manner. We find too, in Kreutzer, a use of 'shared' melody – between voice and pianoforte – leading to a device which can be conveniently called 'anticipation'; the pianoforte phrase anticipates that in the voice, so that the complete melodic curve is shared between the two performers and endless possibilities of meaning and musical variety open out. There is a striking example of it in his setting of Uhland's 'Frühlingsglaube', a poem so well known from Schubert's own setting of it in 1820. This device of 'anticipation' permeates the work of Schubert: a masterly use of it, for the sake of variety and for recreating the spirit of the poet's words, occurs in 'An die Türen', a lyric from Goethe's novel *Wilhelm Meister*, which Schubert set in 1816.

Finally, in reading over these songs of Schubert's predecessors, one is struck by something quite novel: the evolution of a type of melody, attractively simple, and shapely, whose contours arise naturally from the minor scale. The mood achieved is grave and thoughful. If we think of the great arias of Bach and Handel, composed in a minor key, too numerous and well-known to need a reference, we realize that the mood *they* create is grievous or tragic, decidedly deeper and more heart-stricken than the mood of the Zumsteeg school when they compose these songs in the minor key. It is remarkable that if Gluck or Mozart wish to convey similar moods of sadness or grave reflection they composed, as often as not, in a *major* key. The lesser song composers contributed something new in their minor-key *Lieder*, a type of sad-sweet tune which was to lead to some of the most endearing of Schubert's shorter lyrics, songs like 'Wonne der Wehmut', 'Die Mainacht' or 'Erster Verlust'. From Zumsteeg, as an example, here is his setting of Desdemona's 'Willow Song' from Act V of *Othello*.

EX. 1

Das ar - me Kind! Sie sass und sang, an ein - em Baum sass sie Die

Hand ge - legt auf ih - re Brust, dem Kopf ge - stützt auf's Knie.

An attempt has been made here to understand what lay, to a great degree subconsciously, in the young Schubert's mind when his very early attempts at song-writing were behind him, when he began to realize that the music he longed to bring to utterance could be so easily awakened and drawn from him by his response to poetry. Late in 1814 he was prepared. His

11

technical accomplishment was phenomenal (and how unbearably absurd seem the adverse judgements of the nineteenth century on that technical accomplishment). He had seen what other men had tentatively done with the setting of poems to music. He loved and read widely the poetry which a newly awakened literary Germany was producing. And then, in October 1814, during his reading of *Faust*, he encountered Gretchen's words, sung as she sat spinning, heart-sick and afraid. We know the result of that encounter, but whether the result of his reading a poem was a masterpiece like 'Gretchen am Spinnrade' or a song which is negligible, his capitulation to the poet's text was always total. The response, the technical equipment, the strong musical imagination, were there for the poet's service, and it is with the poem in Schubert's hands that we must begin if we want to understand and appreciate to the full the vast treasury of the Schubert songs.

II

THE GOETHE SONGS

Goethe's international reputation as sage, philosopher and dramatist has overshadowed the fact that he is also Germany's greatest lyric poet. The musician who knows him only through the great song writers is at least acquainted with that essential aspect of his work. Schubert's response to the rapturous and spontaneous outpourings of Goethe's lyric genius has produced a collection of songs unrivalled by any similar group in his songs to texts by a single poet. It is only possible to consider here the finest of his Goethe settings – those unmentioned include a few which are worthy of their composer, but also a number which are negligible. Goethe's qualities, to which Schubert instantly responded, are intense sincerity of feeling expressed with unmatched force and clarity of language. This is not to say that the thought is always uncomplicated: in songs such as 'An den Mond' (the second version), 'Prometheus' and 'Grenzen der Menschheit', Schubert has not entirely realized in music Goethe's swift and questing intellect. But when the thought is concentrated and straighforward the composer gives us a song which is flawless and eternally appealing.

The first Goethe song is 'Gretchen am Spinnrade', an incredible realization for so young a composer of Gretchen's fear and heart-break as she sits spinning. The accompaniment suggests the turning wheel by a musically admirable figure, capable of expansion and exploitation, which conventional trills and tremolos (the stock-in-trade of lesser men with spinning-songs) cannot encompass. Gretchen's melodies rise and fall above the whirring wheel, and the climax of the song has won the admiration of musicians ever since it was first heard. As Gretchen thinks of Faust's kiss she is transported; the wheel stops, the music is silent. The resumption of the pianoforte figure to portray the stricken return to her task is musically superb and psychologically profound. The effect of the song is still disturbingly vivid.

Before the end of the year (1814) Schubert set four more Goethe texts including 'Schäfers Klagelied', the first popular example of his 'modified' strophic song. It shows us Schubert using with great charm the minor-key melody referred to on

p. 11, and even when he writes on this modest scale, bringing his song to a picturesque climax. Many of the Goethe songs of 1815 are simple, strophic songs, amongst them the most familiar being 'Nähe des Geliebten' and 'Heidenröslein'. The first of these songs, in which the poet is reminded of his love by the everyday scenes about him, gives us one of Schubert's lovely melodies, rising and falling with inimitable grace; but its most notable feature is the workmanship displayed in the pianoforte prelude. This starts off-key, so to speak, and rises to a harmonic climax for the entry of the voice with the words: 'Ich denke an . . .' ('I think of thee'). 'Heidenröslein' is a gem; its attractive melody needs no elaborate accompaniment and Schubert gives it none. The postlude merely serves to emphasize its simplicity of form. When Ferdinand Schubert, in 1845, produced a set of song-books for use in the Viennese schools, he included 'Heidenröslein'; the education authorities of the city objected to the inclusion of such a song, because of its 'lascivious text'. Fortunately the song can be sung without awareness of such undesirable symbolism in Goethe's poem.[1]

Amongst the modified strophic settings of Goethe's poems in 1815 are three admirable songs. 'Erster Verlust' is an example of that unequalled power by which Schubert gets right under our defences. It sings of the poet's sadness when he contemplates the first love of youth: 'Who can bring back those lovely days of first affection?' The words are set to another of Schubert's sad-sweet melodies in a minor-key. In the middle of the short song the pianoforte joins in with the voice: it is all as simple as can be; but at the words 'my wound' a short chromatic figure stabs in the accompaniment, like a twinge of pain:

EX. 2

[1] This verdict of the Vienna authorities was communicated to me by Father Reinhard Van Hoorickx.

The melody recurs at the close. It is perhaps a sentimental page, but it is elevated by the poet's sincerity and Schubert's heartfelt response.

It is a significant fact that while 'Kennst du das Land?' is the most admired lyric in the German language, not a single setting of it, and there are many, has won the world's regard. Schubert's own setting has never taken its proper place among his Goethe songs, for it is most attractively written: a tuneful treatment in A major of the first two verses, the description of Italy and the Italian mansion, with a change into A minor for the third verse, telling of Mignon's unhappy memories of her journey over the Alps.

The third of these songs of 1815, 'An den Mond', is one of Schubert's rich meditations on Goethe's theme, the longing for a friend's consolation. The song is in A flat, Schubert's nocturnal key, and the natural scenes, a mist-shrouded moon, the full flowing river, are depicted by chromatic and beautifully phrased figures in the pianoforte part. When the poet turns to address the river (an irresistible invitation to Schubert) the rippling figure in the accompaniment leads the music into A flat minor and C flat major, while the more complex thought of the poet produces an extraordinary chromaticism in the vocal part. For the return of the opening music, Schubert modulates back to A flat major, with his usual bewitching effect, and the words about the 'buds and blossoms of Spring' are set to this phrase:

The semiquaver figure marked *a* is associated inseparably in Schubert's mind with Nature, and comes over and over again in his songs whenever the poem touches on natural scenes and occurrences.

The great variety of the Goethe songs of 1815 could be illustrated by two short songs of the period, chosen perhaps from personal liking when so many others claim attention with equal merit. The first is the celebrated 'Meeresstille'. Goethe's picture of the sailor's awe, when in a becalmed ship, is given its perfect musical equivalent; a succession of slow chords, each to be played in deliberate arpeggio so that the sound should ooze up from the depths of the pianoforte like the heave of an oily sea, supports the chromatic phrases of the voice – phrases with a hint of terror lurking beneath the surface. The second is the practically unknown 'Die Spinnerin'. *This* poem might well have been condemned by a strait-laced committee as having a lascivious text – but that is hardly the reason why the song is neglected today. The girl is not actually spinning as she laments her desertion, but the accompaniment is masterly in its oblique suggestion of the spinning wheel. As in 'Gretchen am Spinnrade'. Schubert's devising of a short musical figure for the 'spinning motive' enables him to develop it thoroughly, until it surrounds the girl's plaint with an aura of sound, like the remembered hum of a busy wheel – which also stopped, but this time when a 'handsome young man' appeared on the scene.

The most famous song of 1815 is 'Erlkönig'. I have expressed elsewhere my doubts about the veracity of the anecdote describing its inception. Schubert invariably sketched his songs, and so incredibly well constructed a song as 'Erlkönig' cannot have been an exception to this rule. The phenomenal use of the pianoforte to convey to the listener not only the wild ride through the forest at night, but also the emotions of the fearful child and the anxious father, are beyond praise. Even more remarkable, and this was first pointed out by Sir Donald Tovey in a superb programme note on the song, is the treatment of the pianoforte when the Erlking speaks. During the rest of the song we are observers: we watch the ride, we hear the child's voice and the father's reassuring answers. But only the child hears the Erlking, and the rocking, almost lulling, movement of the pianoforte accompaniment is the child's experience of the motion of the galloping horse, the warm protection of his father's arms, while he trembles at the sinister invitations. When he cries out, we revert to our roles as observers and the clamour of the hoofs, the rush of the wind, break again on our ears. The final page, with the arrival home and the ensuing silence, enables the dreadful simplicity of Goethe's and Schubert's last line to make an overpowering effect. 'Erlkönig' was the first song of Schubert's to be published; it appeared in April 1821 as his Op. 1. At that time, and for a century afterwards, it was considered his greatest song but, magnificent as it is, it is not the whole Schubert, and the Goethe songs which were composed in the following years show even subtler and more refined aspects of his powers than does 'Erlkönig', while still preserving its elements of grandeur and poetry.

'An Schwager Kronos', of 1816, is a song in this great tradition of 'Erlkönig'. Goethe's almost insolent address is to Time as a coach-driver (*Schwager* = brother-in-law, a familiar way of addressing eighteenth-century postilions), yet he touches the heights of lyrical poetry, and Schubert, gripped by the superb lines, produced a fine, confident song. The circling octaves of the accompaniment convey the idea of the galloping horses and the melodies stream above this unceasing movement. The song starts in D minor and the tonality shifts excitedly until the first climax is reached in E flat major. At this point the poet hails with joy the glorious prospects offered by the years ahead and Schubert rises magnificently to the challenge:

EX. 4

It is as if, in the tempestuous ride, we have topped a mountain crest, and endless and spacious vistas stretch before us. A brief moment of repose for the drink at the wayside inn and the horses

17

are whipped up; the song thunders to its end as the posthorn summons the porter at the gate of Hell. The music of the last verse is in D major – Schubert's key of triumphant happiness, and not for one moment does the exhilarating run of the galloping octaves cease. The accompaniment is the most difficult in all Schubert, if taken at the right speed and played articulately. In the same noble vein are the two songs 'Ganymed' (March 1817) and 'Prometheus' (October 1819). The first is an ecstatic greeting to Jove, the all-loving Father, and Schubert's music is as fresh as the spring morning it celebrates. The episodic structure of 'Prometheus' is not wholly successful since inevitably it leads to a disjointed effect. But how superb some of the episodes are! Goethe's hero hurls imprecations at Zeus and Schubert's music takes on the note of scorn and defiance. The opening episode in particular is magnificently written, exploiting a short musical phrase as a link between the recitatives, urging them on to a climax of furious denunciation. The words in which Prometheus taunts Zeus, crying that both of them are fashioned by Time and victims of Fate, are given the boldest and most revolutionary harmonic writing in all Schubert's *Lieder*. The song ends with a peroration in C major, a setting of Prometheus' resolve to breed a race of men *like* him. It is the last of Schubert's settings of Goethe on the grand scale, but before coming to the final group of lyrics, we return to September 1816, and to a consideration of three songs in which the profundity of utterance almost surpasses that of the poems which inspired it. They are the three 'Gesänge des Harfners' (Harper's songs) from the novel *Wilhelm Meister*. The songs show a unity of musical expression partly due to the prevailing mood of A minor, in which key all three songs are set: it is Schubert's key of lost contentment, and the mood of despair persists throughout. 'Wer sich der Einsamkeit ergibt' describes the loneliness of the Harper; the broad phrases have anguished turns in the melodic contours. The closing lines are sung over a descending bass of great poignancy: to English ears it inevitably recalls Purcell's 'When I am laid in earth'. The second song is an even finer piece of work, a setting of 'Wer nie sein Brot mit Thränen ass'. Goethe's cynical despair is transmuted by Schubert's poetical approach into a cry of humanity against the cruelty of Fate. In the first verse the Harper sings that only he who has eaten his bread with tears knows the Heavenly Powers; Schubert's deeply pathetic melody ends unexpectedly in A major and there is a further and maturer use of that stabbing chromaticism he had previously used in 'Erster Verlust':

EX. 5

The words describing the Heavenly Powers, which give us life only to lead us into poverty and suffering, are sung to a recitative in B flat minor but again the cadence softens to A major. The whole passage is then repeated with the vocal phrases highly elaborated and given a more complex accompaniment. The coda is based on the figure quoted in Ex. 5. Schubert's word-repetitions and the seemingly incongruous sweetness of his A major cadences have led to the criticism that he has missed the sting of Goethe's mockery. It is a point worth making. If unswerving faithfulness to the poet's meaning is the first criterion of a song's success, Schubert may, in this case, have erred; but it could be urged in his defence that he was moved by the thought of ultimate consolation, and that he tried to convey this underlying response of his own to the direct statement of Goethe's Harper. 'An die Türen' is sung by the Harper as he begs from door to door; it is a monody devised over a bass of moving crotchets, a direct representation of dragging footsteps, but obliquely suggesting despairing spirits, even falling tears, and eventually they wear down the music to silence and mute grief. There were earlier settings of the first two poems, but these three songs were Schubert's own choice from his various experiments, and he published them in 1821 as his Op. 12.

There is a break of two years after 1819, and when Schubert again returned to Goethe's poetry he composed a group of delightful love-songs. 'Versunken', in which the lover is entranced by his sweetheart's hair and runs his fingers through her 'rich tresses', is not well known, yet Schubert's ripple of harmonies, glistening like the girl's tresses, and his light but ardent melody are very attractive. The two Suleika songs were composed with a superb soprano voice in mind; it is possible that Schubert

19

intended them for the great operatic singer Anna Milder-Hauptmann. The poems are found in Goethe's *West-östlichem Diwan*, a collection of some two hundred lyrics inspired by the current vogue for oriental art and literature, but his authorship has been questioned; the two poems were probably written by his mistress, Marianne von Willemer. In the first song Suleika addresses the east wind which brings messages from her lover. The passion and sweep of the song are new in Schubert, although we find them again later in songs by Mayrhofer ('Auflösung') and Schulze ('Auf der Bruck'). The second Suleika song is an address by the love-sick woman to the west wind, conveying a message to her lover; it does not quite reach the heights of the first song, but remains for all that an admirable example of Schubert's power to evolve long, sustained phrases based on his initial melodic fragments. The most loved of the group of songs is 'Geheimes'; its fame and the affection it has inspired are thoroughly deserved. The characteristic melody, shapely, memorable, and with that underlying wistfulness so rarely absent from Schubert's melodies, is a perfect representation of the lover's rapture. He hugs his secret to himself in the company of his friends, but his joy almost betrays him.

In December 1822 Schubert composed a further four songs to poems by Goethe. 'Am Flusse', a renunciation of love, was exquisitely set; it displays a novel phase in Schubert's songwriting of the early 1820s. He seems to be experimenting in a pure, diatonic style of harmonic colour, eschewing any boldness of modulation or chromatic surprise. The equable flow of the quavers in 'Am Flusse' gives us the calm waters of the river and the resigned mood of the poet. The chromatic tensions which momentarily cloud the D major melody are soon eased and its simple, lovely line re-established as the love-poems are consigned to the 'waters of oblivion'.[1] The most celebrated of the four songs is the ever-fresh 'Der Musensohn'. The son of the Muses pipes and dances over the countryside and Schubert's happiness in this rhapsodic text is infectious. The dancing rhythms and the impetus given to the interlinked melodies by their sudden plunge into contrasting keys make an irresistible song. Soon after the composition of these four songs Schubert wrote 'Wanderers Nachtlied' ('Über allen Gipfeln ist Ruh' '). The music in this short song, only fourteen bars, uses the

[1] There is an earlier setting of 'Am Flusse', dating from February 1815.

20

simplest possible means – a progression of slow chords, a lightly syncopated figure – but they achieve the most moving effect; the full weight of the poet's words, in which the silence and gathering darkness are seen as symbolic of death, is felt in this miraculous page.

The last Goethe songs were written in January 1826. They are settings of Mignon's lyrics from *Wilhelm Meister* and were published as Schubert's Op. 62 in March 1827. The first of the four settings, a magnificent duet sung by Mignon and the Harper, does not concern us here. The three solo songs are 'Heiss mich nicht reden', 'So lasst mich scheinen' and 'Nur wer die Sehnsucht kennt'. All three had been set by Schubert previously, the last one several times, but these 1826 versions eclipse the former ones. In the first poem Mignon hints at the dreadful secret in her past but begs her listeners not to ask her to reveal it. The song is plaintive, moving steadily in E minor with a consolatory change into E major. When Mignon bursts out that only a god could wrest her secret from her, we have that inspired use of recitative which dramatically breaks the even flow and then resumes with renewed pathos. 'So lasst mich scheinen', in which Mignon pleads to be allowed to continue wearing her fancy dress as an angel, uses a richer harmony and chromatic modulation. The key is B major, and there is a surprising move into D major for the climax of the first verse. In the last verse the climax is repeated, but the music this time, in order to enhance the 'deep pain' of the poem, breaks into D minor, an astonishingly harsh move. 'Nur wer die Sehnsucht kennt' is Schubert's farewell to Goethe. No other poem had touched him so deeply: there are, in all, four settings of the verses for solo voice and the last is the finest. The simple, diatonic melody in A minor which opens the song is succeeded, in a thoroughly Schubertian way, by more tortured chromatic phrases. The emotion rises to a climax of despair and grief, and then subsides. The song ends with the same numbed melody as at the start. If we sometimes feel that the final setting of Goethe from Schubert's pen would more fittingly have been on the lines of 'An Schwager Kronos' or 'Prometheus', there is at least a sense of completeness when we realize that 'Nur wer die Sehnsucht kennt', although more modest in scope and simpler in execution, recaptures the mood and once again exhibits the exquisite workmanship of his very first Goethe setting, 'Gretchen am Spinnrade'.

III

SONGS TO TEXTS BY MINOR POETS (1814–22)

Only a writer on *Lieder* would presume to lump together some fifteen literary figures as 'minor poets'; a few of these men are of the stature of Klopstock, Hölty and Uhland, whereas others hardly merit the name 'poet' at all. The term is used merely to distinguish them from major poets like Goethe and Schiller, and to classify conveniently a group of favourite songs written by Schubert between 1814 and 1822.

The years 1815–16, sometimes called the 'Song Years' in books about Schubert, saw his production of something like two hundred and fifty songs. Three poets who dominated his choice of texts during that period were Matthisson, Hölty and Kosegarten. Their homely verses (as we meet them in the songs) are mostly love-poems and Schubert's heart was touched by the romantic verses. Matthisson's best-known poem, because of Beethoven's stately setting of it, is 'Adelaide'. Schubert set it, not very characteristically, in 1814, but shortly afterward he composed a song on another of Matthisson's poems, 'Andenken', which is one of the most charming of the songs which precede 'Gretchen am Spinnrade'; the melody is only slightly changed for each verse, but the accompaniment differs quite considerably. The lover's questions, 'When – how – where do you think of me?', show an early use of the interpolated recitative, quite on the lines of Zumsteeg or Zelter, but already indicating future promise. In April 1816 Schubert composed 'Stimme der Liebe'. His imagination was caught by the sunset clouds and the evening star of the first verse; the poet's love, Laura, makes her appearance only in the last of the strophic verses. The slow, 12/8 movement, with some fine harmonic sequences – D minor A minor: C minor G major – is ardent yet controlled; there is a hint of the first movement of the G major Sonata (D. 894) in this interesting song.

There are altogether some twenty-four settings of poems by Ludwig Hölty. It is an endearing group of songs, because Schubert's response to the rather sentimental but obviously sincere verses of the poet was deeper than to the poetry of either Matthisson or Kosegarten. Two poems are addressed to the moon. The first, 'An den Mond', begins 'Geuss, lieber

22

Mond'; the poet asks the moon to reveal the scene where he was happy with his love. He looks and then finds grief, not happiness, and begs the moon to veil her light. The song was composed in April 1815. It starts with one of Schubert's lovely minor-key melodies; in the space of eight bars the phrases of the tune pass from F minor through C flat minor and B flat minor, before returning to the tonic key; it is an example of the marvellous way in which he never allows the almost outlandish chromatic tensions of his melodic writing to impede the easy, lyrical flow. The second and third verses are composed to a different music, with a change of key, tempo and time-signature. The fourth verse repeats the music of the first. Nothing could be simpler than this formal construction, but in listening to 'An den Mond' one is unaware of it; the effect is of an ardent and impromptu outpouring. The second song is usually called 'Klage. An den Mond'. If the thought is morbid, for the unhappy poet tells the moon that its rays will soon fall on his tombstone, it must be remembered that his words were all too soon fulfilled. Like the previous song, it is one more example of the way in which Schubert's inexhaustible imagination modified the strophic song for the sake of variety and interpretation. Reference was made on p. 9 to Zumsteeg's setting of this poem; Schubert's incomparably finer treatment is shown in his setting. His song starts in F major; the first and second verses are sung to the same melody, but the diatonic harmony of verse 1 is completely changed in verse 2, becoming a highly-charged and chromatic support for the voice, which sings of the poet's apprehension. The third verse is differently composed; it is a D minor episode, grieving as it sings of the poet's tomb.

The well-known 'Seligkeit' is a setting of a Hölty love-poem. The bewitching tunes, one for the pianoforte and one for the voice, make a light-hearted *Ländler* of the lover's joy. Who, having heard it, could forget Elisabeth Schumann's performance of this song? It might have been composed for her. 'Frühlingslied', an enthusiastic greeting to the May-time countryside, inspired one of Schubert's gayest pastorals; it is in the style of a folk-song, but touched with a lyrical poetry which no folk-song possesses.

The poems of Kosegarten made a strong appeal to the young Schubert; between June 1815 and July 1816 he set twenty of them. Then the attraction ceased. Most of the songs are strophic and secondary; we feel that they took Schubert's fancy and that the composing of them answered a need of his to express in music the emotions that they aroused. The songs have considerable variety, ranging from 'Das Sehnen', a short and impassioned song in A minor, true Schubert in every bar, to the stately address to the sunset 'An die untergehende Sonne'. This is an episodic song; by loving and detailed workmanship Schubert redeems what was largely a dutiful response to the poet's formal verses. The most likeable of Schubert's love-songs to Kosegarten texts are the pair known, rather prosaically, as 'An Rosa I' and 'An Rosa II'. The melodies are warm and beautifully poised for the voice, but even more admirable is the way in which Schubert works flawlessly in these two tiny songs to unite the pianoforte figures and harmonies so that they point and complete the vocal phrases. Both songs were composed on that incredible day, 19 October 1815, which saw the birth of nine songs. We cannot leave the Kosegarten songs without a brief mention of one which is sadly neglected—'Die Mondnacht'. It is one of the songs of Schubert's youth which starts pleasantly and mildly enough, and then suddenly takes wing because something in the poet's words fires Schubert's imagination; in this case the 'sparkle of the rain-wet leaves in the moonlight'.

A similar variety is found in the dozen or so settings of Friedrich Klopstock – a more important name in German literature than those of the three poets mentioned above. The best-known song is 'Dem Unendlichen', because it is a singer's piece. The dramatic recitatives at the start give way to bel canto phrases which float above the pianoforte arpeggios, inspired by a typically Klopstockian reference to the 'harp-tones of the Tree of Life'. Two love-poems, both exhibiting Schubert's delicious use of chromatic sequences and picturesque figuration in the pianoforte part, and both with attractive melodies, are 'Das Rosenband' and 'Edone'; they deserve to be better known. Even more neglected is 'Die Sommernacht'. Its full stature is not obvious at first glance, but performed by a singer and pianist who would be prepared to give it more than superficial treatment, its beauty would place it high amongst Schubert's secondary songs. The poet gazes at the glory of a summer night. It reminds him of his dead sweetheart, and only his memories of her give him any pleasure as he looks at the scene. Schubert clearly pored with delight over his text; the opening lines blend recitative and lyrical phrases and these gradually merge, with growing interest in the pianoforte figures, into the closing, streaming melody. The song, marked 'langsam, feierlich', could hardly be sung too slowly.

Late in 1816 Schubert encountered for the first time the poetry of Matthias Claudius. His short, simple verses have given us two of Schubert's celebrated songs. 'Wiegenlied' is a gem among cradle songs and it displays an early use by Schubert of a short musical phrase associated in his mind with 'sleep':

EX. 6

The two adjacent thirds on 'Schlafe, schlafe', bracketed above, form the basis of nearly all the melodies in his many songs to poems dealing with, or touching on, sleep. 'Der Tod und das Mädchen' was composed in February 1817. It has been popular from the first and it was undoubtedly the love felt by his friends for this particular song that inspired him to write variations on it for the D minor String Quartet of March 1824. More substantial settings of Claudius are found in the extremely fine elegy published as 'Am Grabe Anselmos', and in the two exuberant songs, both very different treatments of the same poem 'Ich bin vergnügt', but both so wholly enchanting that it is difficult to decide which is the better. This poem was entitled simply 'Lied' by Claudius, and Schubert's songs are similarly entitled; they are catalogued by Deutsch as 362 and 501. A favourite song to words by Claudius, perhaps with Schubertians rather than with the general public, is 'An die Nachtigall' (D. 497).

From the work of a few minor poets Schubert selected some forty poems for his songs. Each is remembered by only one or two, when Schubert's unaccountable genius was suddenly awakened by their words, so that he penned those dew-fresh melodies which have become part of our musical heritage, or else was moved deeply to produce a song which touches the depths. Salis (to give him his full name: Johann Gaudenz von Salis-Seewis) inspired, among several songs, two which are well known and which exemplify the two extremes in the previous sentence. 'Der Jüngling an der Quelle' is enchanting; the lad wants to forget the girl who has jilted him, but the waters of the spring babble her name continually. Not even among the variety of pianoforte devices in *Die schöne Müllerin* did Schubert strike so happy a representation of gushing water; the A major melody leans towards D minor and A minor, but the girl's name cannot be banished from the memory, and returns triumphantly at the close. 'Ins stille Land' is a solemn contemplation of death. Schubert composed the song in March 1816; he made several copies, the last, quite unknown, as late as August 1823; it is a pity that this last and quite the best variant was never available for the definitive, printed edition. The song foreshadows in a remarkable way not only the mood, but even the melodic contours, of the last Goethe song, 'Nur wer die Sehnsucht kennt'.

Christian Schubart is the author of 'Die Forelle', without doubt one of the most popular of all Schubert's songs in his lifetime, judging from the number of copies he made for his friends and, again, from the fact that he was asked to write variations on the tune; these grace the Pianoforte Quintet in A major, composed two years after the song. The tune of 'Die Forelle' is immediately engaging; its gradual evolution, until it reached the familiar form we all know, is not of merely pedantic interest. The song was composed in 1816 and a fair copy, Schubert's fourth, was written four years later for publication. Each of the four variants shows a slight change, the addition of a dotted note or a melodic turn, until the final, perfect shape was attained. The accompaniment, with its graphic depiction of eddying water, adds its own friendly charm to the song. The middle section, in which the trout is so craftily landed, introduces a mock-serious note, after which Schubert easily recaptures the lyrical mood of the opening.

Another Schubart song, 'An mein Klavier', is deservedly becoming more popular. Its title, regrettably, is gathering two accretions which we should do well to scrape off before they adhere too firmly: 'Serafina', the girl in the poem, was excluded by Schubert from his song and need not be brought back by the pedants, and 'Schubert an sein Klavier' is an entirely unjustified flight by the late A. H. Fox Strangways in his published collection of English translations of Schubert's texts.

A parallel to Salis is found in two songs on poems by J. G.

Jacobi. One, the 'Litanei auf das Fest "Aller Seelen" ', is a universally celebrated and well-loved example of Schubert's mystical songs. The slow and serene melody is supported by broken chords in the accompaniment; the voice part is ornamented with turns and the harmony is highly chromatic. All the essentials are present which could have gone to the making of a sanctimonious page, instead of which Schubert's 'Litanei' is a benediction, and the emotion is never defiled by a trace of sentimentality. Among the half a dozen other Jacobi settings is another, 'Die Perle', which would well repay an occasional performance. The jewel is symbolic, of what the poet is not too clear, but his hero searches the world over for this pearl of great price. Schubert sees the poem as a pilgrimage and the expressive D minor harmonies depict the striding of the searcher through field and forest. Alois Schreiber is the author of 'An den Mond in einer Herbstnacht,' composed by Schubert in April 1818. It is a thousand pities that the poet needed six verses for his nocturnal reminiscences; Schubert's marvellous inspiration at the start declines a little in the middle of this long poem although, fortunately, the text enabled him to conclude by a recapitulation of his opening music. The soft tread of the pianoforte chords, with the lovely snatches of melody above them, comes from the poet's description of the autumnal moon as 'she walks the night in her silver shoon'. Soon after the entry of the voice we have that magical moment when the left hand takes over the work of accompanying leaving the right hand free to point and adorn the words with its own lovely contribution:

EX. 7

The appeal of this song lasts over the years; it gives us that Schubert whom we sometimes conjure up in imagination: alone in his room, transported by the poem in his hands, pouring out the music which rose in his excited mind without thought of performance, publication or fame. It may be a false picture, but it is a heart-warming one.

'Der Wanderer' was composed in November 1816; it is an example of Schubert's episodic structures, derived, through Zumsteeg and Reichardt, from the operatic scena. The poem, by an otherwise unknown writer, G. P. Schmidt, is a conventional utterance by a fashionable literary figure of that day – the wandering exile, an unwelcome stranger wherever he stays his feet. Schubert's song is anything but conventional. The spacious and noble C sharp minor declamation at the start gives way to more measured, songlike passages; the tempo quickens as the wanderer cries out for the scenes and friends of his homeland. At the climax, the question 'O Land, where art thou?' introduces one of Schubert's grandest uses of the recitative which interrupts the movement but thereby raises expectation to a high pitch – and satisfies it. For as the wanderer realizes that he will find no happiness in the present, Schubert is enabled to round off his song with a return to the deep, emotional richness of the start. The appeal of 'Der Wanderer' is not so strong today as it was in Schubert's lifetime and for many decades after his death. The quick episodes are considered inferior to the splendour of the opening; singers could do much to unify this seeming disparity by a careful interpretation of Schubert's marking 'geschwind' ('fast')—there is no need to trivialize these episodes.

Schubert's only setting of the poet Ludwig Uhland is 'Frühlingsglaube'. It is a welcome to spring as the consoler of winter's unhappiness, the reviver of joy in life. At the start the gentle breezes blow and bring the warm, sweet air. Schubert's pianoforte part rustles softly and melodiously, and the voice enters with one of his most moving melodies; it shows a use of the figure quoted in Ex. 3 above, to which Schubert constantly resorted when natural scenes are described in his poetry. At the end of verse 1, when the words 'nun muss sich alles, alles wenden' ('now all must turn out for the best') are sung, he uses characteristically an arabesque, which, from this song, is worth quoting. If the *melody* is looked at first, what harmony is implied by the graceful, diatonic phrase? Surely the simplest? Yet part of the deep appeal of this song and many similar songs is the unobtrusively original and surprising harmonic support which the composer devises for such diatonic tunes:

EX. 8

It is perhaps worth mentioning that 'Frühlingsglaube', a so spontaneous seeming effusion, sounding as if Schubert wrote it in one burst of deeply stirred creative energy, actually exists in four manuscript versions. The first three, of September 1820, show several efforts (in B flat major) to get the prelude settled and the closing cadential phrase formed to his satisfaction. Even then, just before publication, he recalled the manuscript and revised the whole song again; it is this version, in A flat major, which appeared in 1822 as his Op. 20, no. 2.

IV

SONGS TO TEXTS BY ENGLISH POETS

A quite substantial group of Schubert songs consists of settings of texts from English poems and ballads. Ten songs are to words by the Gaelic bard Ossian; his poetry, orally transmitted for centuries, was allegedly written down in translation during the eighteenth century by the Scottish schoolmaster James Macpherson. The Ossian epics were extremely popular all over Europe and a very definite contributory cause of the Romantic movement of the following century. Macpherson wrote a primitive prose, deliberately aping the antiquity of genuine balladry. Various metrical versions, from other hands, were soon published in England, and in Germany both the prose original and the subsequent metrical versions were translated. It is not known whose metrical translation Schubert used. None of his settings, composed between 1815 and 1817, has caught the public fancy; they are in general long, and of a discursive character, but they are full of a haunting tunefulness and the pianoforte parts are vividly picturesque, for the moods and actions of the Ossian characters are inseparably linked with the wild, stormy background of mountain, lake and forest. Long, episodic ballads such as 'Der Tod Oscars' and 'Die Nacht' are for the out-and-out Schubertian, but 'Kolmas Klage' and 'Das Mädchen von Innistore' are both practicable in length and the poet's alternation of tense emotion with relaxed, mystical brooding is perfectly caught by Schubert's music. The finest of the Ossian settings are 'Shilrik und Vinvela' and 'Cronnan'. They are an allied pair: in the first the lovers bid farewell, and in the second Shilrik returns from his campaigning to find Vinvela dead. It is possible that a singer might be deterred from undertaking these songs since they appear to be written as duets. This is not so; they are dialogues, but composed for a single voice. The streaming, chromatic thirds in the accompaniment of 'Cronnan', inspired by the waters of the mountain spring, are magnificently developed at the start and at the close of the song; one is reminded of the middle section in No. 2 of the 'Drei Klavierstücke'.

The settings of poems by Sir Walter Scott are more conventional in form, being largely strophic songs, and they have achieved a popularity denied to the Ossian music. Five of them are based on lyrics selected from *The Lady of the Lake*. Of Ellen's three songs, the third, known as 'Ave Maria', was greatly loved in Schubert's lifetime – his letters and those of his friends contain many references to it. If its extreme popularity, which has frequently taken it down to very low levels of music-making, has led to a slight ostracism amongst *Lieder* singers today, it would be sheer prejudice to deny its inherent beauty, both of vocal melody and of superb workmanship in the accompaniment. Ellen's second song, 'Jäger ruhe von der Jagd' (Huntsman, rest), is attractive and so is the polonaise-like 'Lied des gefangenen Jägers' (Lay of the imprisoned hunts-man); but the long-drawn and rhythmically monotonous 'Normans Gesang' is one of Schubert's least attractive songs. These *Lady of the Lake* songs were composed in the spring and summer of 1825; Schubert hoped that by being published with the English texts they would help to spread his fame in England. 'Lied des gefangenen Jägers' was in fact published in Vienna in two independent versions, with English and German words, but the venture was not successful. Two other settings of Scott, both poems selected from his novels, 'Lied der Anne Lyle' (from *A Legend of Montrose*) and 'Gesang der Norna' (from *The Pirate*), have remained – perhaps deservedly – obscure.

By far the most successful of Schubert's English songs are his settings of Shakespeare's lyrics 'Hark, hark! the lark!' and 'Who is Sylvia?' Here is the true Schubert, the composer of incomparable melody. The first song, with its exuberant greeting to the dawn, uses the same procedure as 'Der Musensohn': a sudden swerve into another key gives unbounded verve to the second verse about the 'winking marybuds'. 'Who is Sylvia?' has a melody of such spontaneity and grace that it seems dry and academic to point out the subtle use of sequence in its balanced structure. A plea might be entered here for the over-looked 'Trinklied'. It is a setting of the drinking-song from Act II of *Antony and Cleopatra*. The robust tune is sometimes quoted unaccompanied; it loses much of its appeal if it is so divorced from its complementary pianoforte part. Together they are tremendously effective.

Two single poems are Pope's 'The Dying Christian to his Soul', which appears in Schubert as 'Verklärung' and Colley Cibber's 'The Blind Boy'. The first was translated by Herder. It is the work of the young Schubert – his tenth extant song – but it is infused with genuine ardour. 'Der blinde Knabe', translated by J. N. Craigher, has to our way of thinking an uncongenial subject. Capell expressed the modern revulsion when he wrote: 'For the sighted complacently to put smooth words into the mouth of the blind, and to make a comfortable song out of unimagined disaster is a sentimentality and an impertinence.' It is a pity, for Schubert's song is delicate and tuneful, and the accompaniment figures derive from those in the voice part as they do in the more famous 'Der Einsame' of the same month.

V

THE PERIOD OF *DIE SCHÖNE MÜLLERIN*

Wilhelm Müller, the author of the twenty poems which form
Schubert's song-cycle *Die schöne Müllerin*, died in 1827. Just
before his death he wrote to a friend: 'Perhaps a kindred spirit
may some day be found, whose ear will catch the melodies from
my words, and who will give me back my own.' It is ironic to
read this sentence, knowing that Müller died quite unaware
how a 'kindred spirit' had already composed those melodies,
and that they would send the poet's words to the four corners
of the earth. Even without Schubert's music to confer such fame,
Müller's work would still have a small place in the annals of
German literature; the two volumes entitled *Poems from the
posthumous papers of a travelling horn-player*, his best work, live
independently of the fact that they are the source of *Die schöne
Müllerin* and the later cycle *Winterreise*. In writing the story of
the young miller and his doomed love for his master's daughter,
Müller used a conventional literary motive of the period. Goethe
himself toyed with the idea and wrote in 1797 to Schiller: 'There
are pretty things of the sort (i.e. lyric conversations) in a certain
older German period, and much can be expressed in the form.
. . . I have begun such a conversation between a lad who is in
love with a miller's maid, and the mill-stream, and hope to send
it soon.'

The mill-stream mentioned by Goethe is an important
'character' in the little drama which Müller related in a series of
short lyrics. Schubert made it even more prominent: its presence
is felt when the words make no mention of it. He composed his
songs between the summer of 1823 and the spring of 1824. By
that time his technical prowess was such that it could answer
every demand of his strong musical imagination. If we force
ourselves to ignore the captivating beauty of the *Müller-Lieder*
and examine the music purely as patterned and constructed
sounds, we cannot pay too high a tribute to Schubert's workmanship.

Each type of his songs is found in the cycle: the strophic, the
modified strophic, the episodic and the 'on-running' or
'durchkomponiert' song. All these forms he had tried before and
in each one he had already written many masterpieces. The only

new aspect of these tried formulae in *Die schöne Müllerin* is the intenser beauty of the voice part, the variety of pianoforte figuration to convey the flowing brook, and, in the preludes, the unerring and immediate evocation of atmosphere or mood. There is as much, or more, to admire in the treatment of short, musical themes within the songs, in the superb use of recitative, and in the harmonic colouring, so delicately and acceptably applied.

The story tells of the tragic impact of first, and unrequited, love on an innocent youth. He bids farewell to his old home in 'Das Wandern'. In 'Wohin?' he meets the brook as it tumbles unharnessed down the hillside, and the melody also 'glideth at its own sweet will', expressing the lad's questions and wondering admiration, without pause. We get the first hint of the mill-wheel in the pianoforte part of 'Halt!', as the mill-house is glimpsed among the alder-bushes and the waters of the brook slow down to the sluice-gates: is this where you lead me? asks the young miller. The next song, 'Danksagung an den Bach', starts with the same question and adds another: you lead me to the miller's daughter? Schubert's flowing G major melody takes a thoughful turn into G minor, and then resumes the major key as the lad decides that hands and heart will now be fully occupied. 'Am Feierabend' gives us a glimpse of life and work at the mill. The stones turn and grind, while the youngster wishes he had a thousand arms to do his work more ably. His thudding heart and the rushing water are blended into a fiery unity, but Schubert's direction should not be overlooked – 'rather fast'. The miller's words of praise and the girl's demure 'Goodnight' are sung to recitatives which suspend the stormy movement, giving a wonderful sense of a summer evening's stillness. 'Der Neugierige' is one of the peaks of the cycle. Its melodies are so transparently simple, yet indescribably beautiful. The progress of Schubert's art in the use of declamation, which gives contrast without disunity, is seen in the phrases where the lad confides to the brook that his whole world hangs on the girl's 'Yes' or 'No'. His passionate declaration of love bursts out in 'Ungeduld'; it is the most popular song in the cycle, in the sense that it is most frequently performed independently. Here more then ever it is necessary to observe the composer's 'somewhat fast'. Most singers rush it off its feet, mistakenly supposing that ardour can best be expressed by speed. The marvellous sequential structure of the melody and even more the supremely fine chromatic harmony which underpins it are lost when the song is sung too quickly. 'Morgengruss' is an idyll of a summer morning. Is the girl shy of his approach or indifferent to it? The music poses the questions but does not answer them. The next two songs, 'Des Müllers Blumen' and 'Thränenregen', charming examples of Schubert's lesser love-songs, suffer perhaps because their strophic form leads to much repetition. The convention of singing all the verses of each one, though praiseworthy, is possibly misguided. In 'Mein', we reach the happy climax of the love-story, although the young miller may be self-deceived. He calls on the brook, and all Nature, to rejoice with him in his happiness. A technical point may be mentioned here. It becomes obvious in these mill-songs, although there is plenty of evidence both before and after *Die schöne Müllerin,* that another of those musico-literary images which enrich Schubert's *Lieder* is the association of water with themes based on the notes of the common chord. The brook is addressed thus in *Mein:*

EX. 9

Throughout the cycle this imagery can be found.

'Pause' is the finest of the twenty songs. The development of the melodic germ in the prelude, and of the 'lute-motive' which heralds the words 'meiner Sehnsucht' are fascinating in themselves, quite apart from the thoughtful melodies which they accompany. But at the close of the song we get one of the most masterly uses in the whole of Schubert of the questioning recitative. The lover's lute hangs on the wall; is this the end of his anxiety? and the prelude to new songs?

EX. 10

The modulations and the poignant harmonies express these emotions wonderfully – but still leave the questions unanswered.

The happiness, continuing in the likeable little song 'Mit dem grünen Lautenbande', receives its first set-back with the coming of the green-clad huntsman. 'Der Jäger' is an agitated, scherzo-like song, depicting the young miller's fierce resentment. In 'Eifersucht und Stolz' the brook flows stormily, reflecting the despair of the lover who knows his sweetheart to be unfaithful. The heartbreak in the music as he asks the brook not to betray his fears, but to pretend that he is happy, could come from no pen but Schubert's. The next two songs tell of the miller's obsession with the colour green; the green of the lute-ribbon associated with his love, and the green of the huntsman's clothes which symbolize his jealousy and despair. 'Die liebe Farbe' is a threnody on the death of his happiness. In 'Die böse Farbe' he wants to destroy the green of fields and trees and leave the world outside the maid's window as white as death. The unification in this song of different ideas, the urge to destroy, the hunting horn, the maid gazing from her window, is admirable;

Schubert's scheme for obtaining this unity is set out, if we look for it, in the four bars of the pianoforte prelude. 'Trockne Blumen' is a favourite song; its pathos is made more appealing by the sad little cadence that echoes the phrases of the voice.[1] The brook consoles the lover in 'Der Müller und der Bach' and he seeks peace in its waters. The lullaby sung by the brook over the dead lover, 'Des Baches Wiegenlied' is gentle and melodious. Here also the five stanzas are too many; not only would the song itself gain if a few of the verses were omitted, we should be spared some of Müller's embarrassing imagery.

One of Schubert's earlier songs, which strikes a prophetic note for *Die schöne Müllerin*, is Schiller's 'Die Götter Griechenlands', composed in 1819. The poet regrets the passing of the golden age, and longs for its return. Schubert depicts the happy past in A major, the sigh for its return in A minor. He re-used the striking figure in the prelude for the *minuetto* of the String Quartet in A minor (D. 804); it may possibly be a delibe- rate reference to the Schiller poem – a longing for past happiness. Schiller is the author of a number of Schubert's songs, but few of them are frequently sung. The most powerful is 'Gruppe aus dem Tartarus', in which the vision of tormented souls in hell is given by Schubert a harsh, discordant setting. The last of his Schiller songs is the strangely neglected 'Dithyrambe', of 1824. When the gods of classic myth appear, says Schiller, they never come alone: the mind sees them all. But he first mentions Bacchus, and Schubert's bacchic ode is splendidly rhythmic and tuneful.

Matthäus von Collin is the author of 'Der Zwerg', a ballad using those sham characteristics of mediaeval lore which have come to be dubbed 'Gothic'. The ship sails into the sunset and the dwarf strangles the unfaithful queen; to us it is sheer hocus- pocus, but Schubert saw only the enacted tragedy. The right hand sustains its tremolo chords throughout the song, while stark figures in the bass convey not only the sense of sea and space, but develop musically almost in terms of the Wagnerian leitmotive. The favourite song by Collin is 'Nacht und Träume'. The key is B major and darkness is depicted by the slow, rocking semiquavers in the bass of the pianoforte; in the graceful rise

[1] Is it beyond credence that Wagner was, no doubt subconsciously, indebted to this song? He uses the same cadence and, in fact, in the same key, for Brünnhilde's 'War es so schmählich?' in Act III of *Die Walküre*.

and fall of the sustained vocal phrases we hear the greeting to night, the bringer of dreams. There is a sudden change of key to G major, a device of which Schubert never tires, and yet, at the same time, one to which he never fails to impart a sense of surprise and spontaneity; it leads to the second verse in which the singer regrets the break of day. The approach to the new key was sudden but its quitting is slow; the harmonies pass through extreme keys as if to present the unwelcome tasks of day. The return to B major, as night falls again, has a hushed serenity. There is much in Schubert which equals the beauty of these two pages, but little which surpasses them.

Five poems by Friedrich Rückert were set to music by Schubert in 1822–3. All five are in his finest lyrical vein and are very popular. 'Greisengesang' is the fireside meditation of an old man, who consoles his loneliness with memories. Schubert's bare B minor unisons at the opening soften to B major harmonies as the man's mind fills, so to speak, with images from the past. 'Lachen und Weinen' is a complete contrast; the picture of the young girl in love, one moment deliriously happy, the next miserably crying, is beautifully drawn by the skimming F major melody, with its swerve into F minor and – as if the breath were caught by a sob – back into F major. In 'Sei mir gegrüsst' the lover pours out his greeting to an absent sweetheart. Schubert's skill in modulating to distant keys for the varying moods of the impassioned greeting, while returning each time to his tonic key (B flat major) for the refrain: 'I greet you, I kiss you' is musically admirable; yet the five verses sprawl somewhat, and the song needs every art of the singer if it is not to grow monotonous. The last two Rückert songs are masterpieces. 'Du bist die Ruh', like 'Der Neugierige' and 'Nacht und Träume', achieves its effect by the simplest of means; its accompaniment could hardly use fewer notes, and the balanced structure of the melody could serve as a model in a text-book on composition. Yet the effect is of unearthly serenity. In the third verse there is a slight chroma-tic change in the melody which opens up a new world of musical feeling and never fails in its effect. The melody rises slowly, note by note, to its climax, a testing phrase for the singer's technique. Schubert repeats the passage, but obtains variety by small and attractive changes in the accompaniment. In most editions of the song a note in the repetition of the ascending scale is changed. The alteration may have been simply a misprint in the first edition, but it has become established. Since Schubert's own manuscript of 'Du bist die Ruh' is lost, it is impossible to decide which of the two versions is the correct one. 'Dass sie hier gewesen' is an example *par excellence* of Schubert's power to re-create in music the poem which has so deeply impressed him. Not only the beauty of the melody, the poetic figures in the pianoforte accompaniment, the piquant and advanced harmonic colouring, which are all there in the service of the poet: there is also a union of words and music which is deeper than these more surface attractions. 'That the breeze brings fragrance', sighs the poet, 'tells me that you were here.' Schubert clothes the opening words with an ambiguous harmony, reserving his definite C major tonality for the poet's concluding statement: 'that you were here':

EX. 11

The song continues in this noble style to its quiet and moving close.

At this period he composed 'Auf dem Wasser zu singen'; the poem is by Count Leopold Stolberg. The song derives its captivating accompaniment from a small phrase in the voice part. The words 'spiegelnden Wellen' ('mirroring waves') awoke in Schubert's mind a falling figure like a tumbling wave:

39

Mässig geschwind

pp Mit - ten im Schim - mer der spieg - eln - den Wel - len

R.H.

The buoyant and rippling accompaniment, inspired by the figure,
is so attractive that it could almost stand alone – another
Moment musical. Schubert's key signature is A flat major, but
in fact his melody is in the minor key; at the end of the verse, the
words describe the sunlit waves dancing round the boat, and the
major key, held back for so long, is introduced with bewitching
effect.

The spring of 1825 was for Schubert an interlude between a
period of uncongenial teaching duties in the service of the
Esterházy family and a prolonged holiday in the beautiful
countryside of Upper Austria. His time was occupied in Vienna
by a round of social activities, the meeting of many prominent
artists and patrons of the arts, and the increasing demands of
the very popular *Schubertiaden* – evenings devoted to the
performance of his songs. His friend, the baritone Johann
Michael Vogl, was an invaluable interpreter at these functions,
and another singer, whose voice and interpretative powers
greatly appealed to Schubert, appeared in his circle in those
days: the young actress, Sofie Müller. To her, without doubt,
we owe the creation of 'Die junge Nonne'. The poem is by
J. N. Craigher, whose name we have already met; he was the
translator of 'Der blinde Knabe'. It tells of a novice, who
contrasts present peace of mind with a stormy past, which she
likens to the actual storm raging outside the convent walls. Here
are all the elements which go to the making of a Schubertian
masterpiece. His setting is in F minor and the soft tremolando
chords of the pianoforte part are meant to suggest the muffled
noise of the storm as it would be heard by the nun in her secluded
cell. The dynamic rarely rises above pianissimo throughout the
song. The poem opens with the nun's words: 'How the storm roars
through the tree-tops!' Schubert set the words to a short musical

phrase; he must have realized at once the possibilities of development inherent in the thematic figure. It is used in the bass of the accompaniment, adding a new dimension to his storm-scene and, at the same time, giving shape and substance to his shifting harmonic scheme. An admirable feature of the opening two pages is the way in which the continuity of the nun's remarks is broken; during her silences we hear the distant thunder and realize her growing awe at the severity of the storm. In the next verse, when she thinks of her unhappy past, her mood changes, and the phrases are sung in an unbroken line. The music modulates to a confident and melodious passage in F major; the convent bell is heard, and the nun's exalted 'Alleluja!' brings the song to a peaceful close.

During the same month (February 1825) Schubert composed two well-loved songs on texts by an obscure poet, Carl Lappe. 'Im Abendrot' is a hushed prayer to God, inspired by the emotional response of the poet to the beauty of the sunset. It is another song from the Schubert of 'Wanderers Nachtlied' and 'Litanei'; the music calls for singing of noble and sustained tone.[1] 'Der Einsame', like 'Greisengesang', is a fireside picture, but its more homely and varied details bring all kinds of musical delights into the song; a semiquaver figure from the singer's part gives the pianist a chance to illustrate the shrilling of the crickets, or the sparks from the embers:

EX. 13

[1] It is regrettable that nearly all singers use an edition of 'Im Abendrot' which has a corrupt version of the melody at the words: 'eh' es zusammenbricht'. The authentic, and greatly preferable, melodic form can be found in the Breitkopf Complete Edition.

With a touch of canon between voice and pianoforte the singer renounces the outside world, and the broad phrases at the end exemplify the contentment of the solitary figure secluded in his room.

VI

SONGS TO TEXTS BY HIS FRIENDS

Among Schubert's friends were several true poets, but most of the members of his circle wrote verses. He composed some two hundred songs to texts by his friends, and his selection from their work was prompted by personal liking – Grillparzer, the most eminent of the poets, is the author of only one song, Mayrhofer of forty-seven.

Schubert's closest friend was Franz von Schober, the author of twelve songs. His poem 'An die Musik' was set by Schubert in March 1817; it is perhaps his best-loved song. Schober offers a thanksgiving to music, the 'gracious art', and Schubert is absorbed by the poem. His music is tranquil and single-hearted. It is an expression of the gratitude aroused in the composer by his beloved art, not a display of it. There are no extravagances of colour or transitions to other keys, the D major tonality is unclouded. The melody is accompanied by simple, repeated chords in the right hand, while the left hand echoes the vocal phrases. Towards the end of the song the bass rises chromatically to support the emotional climax of the song, and no climax could be more gentle and restrained. The final phrase of the melody, composed presumably for the first verse, is indelibly associated in the minds of musicians with the words of the second verse which ends the song: 'du holde Kunst, ich danke dir' ('Thou gracious art, I thank thee'). In listening to 'An die Musik' it is hard to believe that Schubert did not write both words and music, so perfect a whole is his achievement in this wonderful song.

The ecclesiastic, J. L. Pyrker, Patriarch of Venice, is the poet of two songs in Schubert's grandest style. The poems, 'Die Allmacht' and 'Das Heimweh', were encountered at a happy moment. In the summer of 1825 the composer, with Vogl as his companion, spent a holiday in the countryside surrounding Lake Traun in Upper Austria; he was enchanted by the beauty of mountain and lake, finding restoration of health as well as mental exhilaration. This renewal of body and spirit is poured out in the rapturous music he wrote for the two songs. 'Die Allmacht' sings a hymn of praise to the Creator and is full of glorious Schubertian melodies; 'Das Heimweh', almost its

43

equal from a lyrical point of view, is an even finer example of the composer's gift for thematic development. The pianoforte prelude could easily be the opening of a sonata; the strong, unison theme in A minor, inspired by the poet's reference to the Alpine crags, is used ingeniously in voice and pianoforte as Schubert would have used it in his instrumental works. The almost nonchalant ease in the writing to obtain variety and cohesion can be seen as the voice enters:

EX. 14

The second verse tells of the Alpine lad's homesickness for his cottage in the 'green, sweet-scented meadows'. The music starts modestly enough, with a delicious little tune in the accompaniment as counterpoint to the vocal phrases; but as the poem continues with allusions to the dark firs and the towering crags, Schubert's genius takes over. The little counterpoint expands and develops until it dominates the whole scene, thundering out in widespread chords and leading the music into remoter and darker keys. The gradual recession from this climax is again reminiscent of the Schubert sonata: it recalls the transitional passage at the end of his development section. A brief and scherzo-like episode follows and the final pages recapitulate the minor theme of the start. Even now the excited mind of the composer is not content with mere repetition; the verse describes the irresistible summons of the mountains and Schubert finds yet more possibilities of musical illustration in his theme. 'Das Heimweh' is not in the forefront of Schubert's most famous or most loved songs, but one can return to it again and again and find it to be one of his most remarkable essays in song-composition.

A group of songs by his friend Franz von Bruchmann is more modest in scope. 'Im Haine' sings of the consolation of summer sunshine falling through the fir-trees; Schubert's lilting music embodies the thoughts of the idle dreamer; the song is in A major, his key of contentment. The finest of the Bruchmann songs is 'Am See', with the most attractive representation of rolling, breaking waves in all Schubert's pianoforte music. Both in this song and in 'Im Haine', the composer's art in extending his melodic line to accommodate the poet's thought shows his remarkable technical growth in the early 1820s: this extension could be called 'linear development', a feature of his songs which becomes more and more important as the years pass.

The two brothers Schlegel are famous as translators into German of the plays of Shakespeare. Their own poetry is largely forgotten; most of it lives in the songs which Schubert composed on their poems. The older brother, August Wilhelm, is the author of ten of Schubert's songs; the best known is the charming 'Lob der Thränen', a song whose dance-like melody holds the interest throughout the four stanzas. The use of an independent prelude, artfully designed to make the entry of the voice complete it, reminds us of 'Nähe des Geliebten'. The younger brother, Friedrich, appealed more strongly to the composer. There are settings of sixteen of his poems; nearly all of them are well-known and a few are very popular. The range is extraordinary. At one end of the scale there is the long and magnificent 'Im Walde' (also called 'Waldesnacht'), a meditation at night in the forest, full of Schubertian splendours but protracted beyond all reasonable limits. 'Das Mädchen' and 'Die Rose', on the other hand, are intimate songs; the delicate melodies are the be-all and end-all of each one, and the tenderness of the sentiments is expressed by Schubert with characteristic transitions from major to minor key and back again. In 'Fülle der Liebe' Schubert is deeply moved by the bereaved lover's passionate grief and there is much to admire in the harmonic resource and striking modulations. But the song fails, and the fault lies in Schlegel's prosody, which never allows Schubert's melody to take wing: it comes in short, broken phrases which finally grow tedious. But the song did serve its purpose, for surely we owe to it a great instrumental movement—the *con moto* of the D major Pianoforte Sonata, composed the same month.

Franz von Schlechta, an aristocratic friend of Schubert's, is the author of half a dozen songs. His 'Widerschein' is a likeable poem. A young fisherman waits on the bridge for his sweetheart, gazing down into the water. Unnoticed she approaches him and looks over his shoulder. The sudden appearance of her face, reflected in the water below him, so startles him that he nearly falls into the river. Schubert's setting is delightful; the waiting, the tender anticipation, the girl's reflection in the rippling water, the shock of surprise, are all sketched with the lightest of touches. If any proof were needed of the subtle union in Schubert's songs of words and music, 'Widerschein' provides it. After its composition in 1819 it was published as a supplement to a periodical. The poet then revised his text quite considerably. The altered text was fitted below Schubert's melody for the first edition of 1832 and many charming details of illustration are thereby completely lost. The most popular of the Schlechta songs is 'Fischerweise', possibly about the same two young lovers. The vocal cadences are echoed by the pianoforte in typically Schubertian fashion, but this time the imitation is so charmingly contrived that it can convey both the fisherman's joy in his pursuits and his lightly cynical comments on the wiles of womankind.

The poems of his friend Mayrhofer made by far the deepest appeal to Schubert. He was a man of introspective temperament, pessimistic in outlook, but seriously dedicated to his art; apart from Schubert's selection from his poems, his work is forgotten. Not one of the forty-seven songs is negligible, but it is impossible to consider all of them here. The twenty or so which are included in the popular anthologies divide roughly into three groups, although the long, episodic ballad 'Einsamkeit' cannot be conveniently placed in any of them.

The first group consists of settings by Schubert of poems inspired by the myths and legends of classical antiquity. Goethe, of course, is incomparable in his treatment of what was then so fashionable a literary pursuit and Mayrhofer can only limp behind. The best-known of these classical songs are 'Memnon' and 'Der zürnenden Diana'. The poet likens himself to the famous statue of Memnon, which at sunrise was reputed to utter a musical note. His thought is complicated to the point of obscurity and Schubert can seize only on the more obvious poetic statements, the painful loneliness, the bliss of poetry, the snakes which gnaw at the poet's heart and the solitary star which symbolizes his soul. The song starts with an evocation of the darkness before dawn breaks, and the meditation on solitude is set to a sombre recitative in B flat minor. As the sun rises the music modulates to a radiant and ecstatic F major for the address to poetry. A tortured and chromatic passage depicts the poet's grief and futile hopes, and the song ends with a broad, tranquil episode in D flat major as the symbolic star is glimpsed in the heavens. Admiration rather than affection is one's response to 'Memnon'. It is a remarkable instance of the way in which Schubert's musical thought can be permeated by a single melodic phrase, in this case the last bar of the vocal melody. The whole of 'Memnon', in all its varied assembly of lyric, recitative and accompaniment, springs ultimately from this one short phrase. The appeal of 'Der zürnenden Diana' has faded somewhat. The self-dramatization of the youth, shot by an arrow from the vengeful Diana's bow, is unreal, and something of its artificiality has crept into Schubert's music; the buoyant invention of the opening pages flags as the song proceeds.

The second group contains seven substantial songs, each of them occasionally sung in recitals although none of them is a first favourite. 'Auf der Donau' presents the flowing of the river Danube as symbolic of the passing of Time – Time the destroyer. A graceful phrase rises and falls on the pianoforte to represent the drifting boat, and on the subsequent richly musical development of this figure Schubert builds his song. 'Untergang' ('dissolution'), three times repeated, ends the song. The sentiments in 'Auflösung' are even more despondent, for the poet bids farewell to earth and sun and welcomes the end of existence. Schubert ignores, or fails to catch, this pessimistic message; he is transported by the opening words 'Veil thyself, O sun!' and pours out a radiant apostrophe to sun and earth which really nullifies the poet's morbid desires. A surge of arpeggios in the accompaniment gathers and subsides from beginning to end of the song and the voice soars ecstatically. There is a surprise on the last page: against the soft shimmer of the keyboard tremolos, which seems to mark the end of the song, the voice sings the ominous phrase 'Geh' unter,Welt!' ('dissolve, Earth'). 'Freiwilliges Versinken', in which Mayrhofer addresses the setting sun, shows how Schubert's art in combining recitative and song has forged a flexible vehicle for the expression of his thought. This song, with its declaimed phrases and decorated pianoforte part, holds the promise of 'Der Doppelgänger'. 'Nachtstück' opens grandly but, like 'Der zürnenden Diana', its attraction has faded and for the same reason. It was once very popular, for it does offer the baritone admirable opportunities for poetic declamation and effusive cantilena; but the closing words are insincere and Schubert, in dealing with them, becomes commonplace.

The third group of Mayrhofer settings contains the shorter, favourite songs, some of them extremely popular. Foremost is the utterly delightful 'Nachtviolen', a flower-song of great charm. The little figure in the accompaniment, like a chime of bells on which the name of the flower is rung, sounds throughout. Equally popular is the 'Lied eines Schiffers an die Dioskuren'. It is a solemn, hymn-like song, in which a boatman invokes the aid of the twin stars. The noble melody of the first stanza utters the prayer. In the pianoforte there is a sensitive use of the 'anticipation' device; it contributes to the musical form, but also to the idea that the boatman is seeking in his mind for the phrases of his prayer. The votive offering of the oar comes in the last stanza; the melody is now sung without a break, for the boatman no longer hesitates as he makes his promise. The fresh accompaniment to this verse, with its billowing bass arpeggios, adds to the picture of a confident oarsman. Two earlier songs on Mayrhofer poems are 'Der Alpenjäger' and 'Erlafsee', both composed in 1817. The former tells of an Alpine hunter who, in spite of his vigorous pursuits, cannot forget his sweetheart, waiting at home. Schubert depicts the activities in a swinging F major tune, the thought of the girl in F minor, with an entrancing, unexpected and wholly characteristic modulation into D major. 'Erlafsee' is a word-picture of the lake in Lower Austria near the shrine of Maria-Zell; the music is a pastoral, 6/8 movement, with some charming imitation between the voice and the treble of the pianoforte part.

The last Mayrhofer songs were composed in March 1824, and possibly the last of them all was 'Abendstern'. The poet's star is Love, which shines alone in the sky, shunning, and shunned by, her companions. His questions are set in A minor, the star's replies in A major, with a pathetic droop into A minor. It is one of the most delicately written of all Schubert's songs. The harmony uses the device of 'suspension' – a feature of many of Schubert's 'star' songs; in 'Abendstern' its novel use gives the song its own highly individual character. Schubert's farewell to Mayrhofer, in this exquisite miniature, could hardly be more endearing.

A young man whose literary ambitions brought him into the Schubert circle was J. G. Seidl. The Seidl songs are mostly from 1826; the four which were composed in that year are all of fine quality although only 'Das Zügenglöcklein' is at all popular. A song in Schubert's 'striding' idiom, of which he wrote several, is 'Der Wanderer an den Mond'. The G minor tread of the accompaniment swings into D minor and G major, and its unflagging rhythm persists all through the song; the melodies are pleasantly diversified as Seidl's wanderer first greets the moon, then envies her, for wherever *she* roams, she is always at home. Seidl has a place peculiarly his own in the list of Schubert's poets, for, as we shall see later, he is the author of Schubert's last song.

VII

THE PERIOD OF *WINTERREISE*

A new feature becomes apparent when we consider the songs of
Schubert's last years. He encountered for the first time the
work of several poets, each with a strongly individual style.
The individuality is reflected in Schubert's settings and markedly
differentiates the various groups of songs. One of the first of
these highly distinctive groups is found in the songs to poems
by Ernst Schulze. There is a certain manly utterance in the
works of this young poet, although their moods are sombre;
Schubert's music takes its tone from this new manner. All ten
of the Schulze songs were composed in the year between March
1825 and March 1826. The greater Schubert is found in the two
songs 'Auf der Bruck' and 'An mein Herz', but in spite of some
magnificent music the songs are a little too long to have won the
regard they deserve. The same fault is found in 'Im Walde'
(D. 834) and 'Lebensmut' (D. 883). The pianoforte figures
devised for the accompaniment persist from beginning to end of
each song, and although Schubert introduces endless variety
within his chosen scheme, monotony is not avoided. It is a
feature not only of the Schulze songs, but of many songs in the
middle 1820s. There are less protracted and more likeable
settings of this poet. 'Tiefes Leid' and 'Über Wildemann' are
essays in a new style for Schubert; the tragic love, its pain made
more unendurable by memories, drew from him a subtler blend
of the major and minor modes. The wild, D minor octaves of
'Über Wildemann', typifying the storm-wind on the mountain
tops, soften magically to the A major episode when the poet
addresses love as the May-time of life.

The thought of the poet in 'Der liebliche Stern' is not too
clear – is his star love? – but the poem refers to all kinds of
natural beauties. Schubert clothes these more concrete images
with a series of melodies drawn from his initial theme and they
pass delightfully through a succession of changing keys. The
loveliest of the Schulze songs is 'Im Frühling'. If 'Der liebliche
Stern' gives us Schubert's art in the linear development of a
song-theme, 'Im Frühling' goes further; it is frankly a set of
variations on the song-theme. The stanza-variations grow more
complex as the pianoforte exploits devices of syncopation and

arpeggio. The climax is reached in the G minor variation for verse 3, and at the words 'Only love remains, love and grief!' Schubert achieves an almost unbearable poignancy:

EX. 15

The Schulze songs prepare us a little for the advent of *Winterreise*.

Schubert's second song-cycle on poems by Wilhelm Müller, the twenty-four songs of *Winterreise*, was composed between February and October 1827. The linking narrative of the songs is more vague than in the earlier cycle, partly because it is in the nature of an epilogue to past events, and partly because the poet's final and more logical sequence of poems was unknown to Schubert until he had completed the first twelve songs.

The wintry landscape through which the embittered lover wanders is a different world from that in *Die schöne Müllerin*. In the first song, 'Gute Nacht', he bids farewell to the house where his faithless sweetheart lies sleeping and walks without aim or plan into the night. The threnodic, D minor harmonies and the serious phrases of the melody depict the pain of the departing lover, without touching the misery and anguish which he will later experience. The D major change for the words 'I will not disturb your dreams' is profoundly moving. As he walks from the house the weathervane on the roof seems to him to be a symbol of the fickle heart within; 'Die Wetterfahne' is a picture in music of the vane twisting in the night-wind, and of the satirical bitterness which seizes the man's mind. The falling tears of 'Gefror'ne Thränen' and the uncontrolled grief of 'Erstarrung' display his increasing pain as the memories burn. 'Erstarrung', with its whirl of C minor triplets, calls to mind 'Über Wildemann', especially when the music softens into the major key; this episode describes the happiness experienced when the fields, now deep in snow, wore their summer beauty. 'Der Lindenbaum', the most popular of the *Winterreise* songs, makes its full effect only in the cycle itself. The wanderer stands beneath the bare branches of the tree, dreaming of the leafy summer and of his love. Schubert's song is in E major 'his key of dreams and consolation, and the lovely melody breathes of both. The tears flow again in 'Wasserflut'; they scald his eyes – the chromatic semitone with which Schubert depicts the throb of pain stabs in the pianoforte part – but in the snow they freeze; when they melt, sings the lover, and flow past his dear one's house, they will scald again. The next song, 'Auf dem Flusse', with its splendid balance between the intellectual development of musical theme and the integrity of its emotions, recalls 'Pause' in the earlier cycle. The wanderer stands on the river bank and the frozen water arouses his wonder; how still the once rushing torrent has become. The melody, a simple theme in E minor, suddenly drops at the words 'how still' into D sharp minor. It is an extraordinary change of key and produces an effect of immobility, as if the music, like the water, has frozen:

EX. 16

sehr leise

Fluss, wie still bist du ge - word - en

ppp

He carves his sweetheart's name in the ice and realizes that underneath the torrent still rages; so passion still rages in his frozen heart. These words are sung to grievous, broken snatches of melody but the wonder of the song resides in the accompaniment. The E minor theme of the opening is used as a supporting bass figure, extended through a remarkable series of key-changes; the unity of the song is preserved by its continuous, onward movement, and it adds its own significant contribution to the emotional outcries of the despairing lover.

'Rückblick', another song of unhappy reminiscence, is an agitated movement in G minor, with interludes in G major for the remembered past. The thrusting, irregular melody gives the frantic outbursts of the lover their perfect expression. The aimless wandering leads to a rocky cavern; he has been beguiled there by the 'Irrlicht' (will-o'-the-wisp). The cavernous rocks are suggested by the stark, B minor octaves in the prelude, and the cry that each sorrow finds its grave is set to an anguished, chromatic cadence. 'Rast' is a short, strophic song telling of the night spent in a friendly charcoal-burner's hut; the wanderer's wounds burn more fiercely as he rests in the silence than when he was tramping through storm and snow. He dreams of the spring and his love; the dream and the bitter awakening are told in 'Frühlingstraum'. A delicious, lilting tune in A major describes the dream; the winter dawn is harsh and discordantly declaimed. The wonder of the song is in its exquisite close; the melody, again in A major, is grave and beautifully phrased. Dream and reality are wonderfully caught in these contrasted tunes. 'Einsamkeit', a short song in D minor, paints with its light scoring a picture of frost and a clear, winter sky. The wanderer cries out against the stillness: he could more easily bear his utter misery in a raging storm.

Part II of *Winterreise* opens with 'Die Post'. It is frequently sung apart from the cycle, since the poem is self-explanatory. The posthorn sounds in the E flat major prelude and the heart-break over the non-appearance of the love-letter, an episode in E flat minor, is beautifully welded into the rhythmic fanfares of the music. The lover's grief and the continual probing of his wounds lead to madness; the true cause, the jilting by the girl, is forgotten and no longer mentioned in the poems, In 'Der greise Kopf' and 'Die Krähe', illusion and reality are hard to separate. Frost turns the wanderer's dark hair white and he thinks he has grown old overnight; the crow which flies after him is waiting to pick flesh from his bones. Both songs are in C minor; the mournful little tune in 'Die Krähe' descends with the utmost simplicity through an octave and we stare in wonder at Schubert's power of creating such haunting beauty from so simple a handling of the notes of the scale. The single notes of the bass are in unison with the voice, a device to which Schubert resorts to convey the bleakness of a natural scene. 'Letzte Hoffnung' is one of those songs in which Schubert's pianoforte part is uncannily picturesque; the music is almost visual in its intensity. A few withered leaves flutter on the tree; a rapid, two-note figure sounds, and echoes, pianissimo, on the keyboard and we see the shudder of the skeleton branches. One leaf is taken by the crazed wanderer as a token; it falls to the ground and his hope dies. 'Im Dorfe' is the song of the second night. He listens to the growling dogs and we hear the rattling of their chains in the long bass trills of the pianoforte; he mocks at the sleeping villagers with their dreams of happiness: 'I am finished with dreams, why should I sleep?' The lovely melody is heavy with tears and despair. Morning breaks in storm; the wanderer in 'Der stürmische Morgen' shouts his welcome; winter and storm give him a morning after his own heart. The disordered fancies continue. 'Täuschung' tells of his wandering towards a distant light. Schubert cannot make much of this indefinite poem. He writes a dream-like, dancing song in A major, which never rises above *piano*, to convey the atmosphere of fantasy and hallucination. The lover passes a graveyard and to his mad fancy it seems like an inn, where the rooms are full and the innkeeper inhospitable. This morbid idea is related in 'Das Wirtshaus'. The song is in modified strophic form; the slow F major tune serves for the description of the crowded graves, the seeking for rest; it changes to F minor for the rejection. 'Mut' is a brave attempt, born of frenzied effort, to face destiny with courage. The song is vigorously composed; the vocal phrases, flung out, so to speak, in the teeth of fate, alternate with clanging pianoforte interludes. Sung as part of the cycle (it is occasionally sung independently) it should suggest bravado. Another illusion is described in 'Die Nebensonnen'; the wanderer sees three suns in the sky. To him they are symbolic of three suns in his life – two have set, and now he awaits the setting of the third. The symbolic meaning of the first two 'suns' is a matter for conjecture, but the third is obviously his life. Schubert's song is again in A major, but 'Die Nebensonnen' is more substantial and attractive than 'Täuschung'. The final song, which ends the winter journey, is 'Der Leiermann'. It is a miraculous composition and we cannot be too grateful that Müller's inspired ending gave Schubert this opportunity for closing the tragedy with so superb a song. The wanderer meets a beggar; against the drone of the man's hurdy-gurdy and its thin, tinkling tune, the wanderer sings his greeting and his resolution to go with him. The two depart together; we seem to see them disappearing into the snow and darkness. Is the hurdy-gurdy man another of Müller's symbolisms? However we interpret the poem, the music has a sublime clarity and all-sufficiency.

Two songs from this year could hardly offer a greater contrast to the tragic *Winterreise*. 'An die Laute' is the only popular song of the three which Schubert composed on poems by J. F. Rochlitz. The lute is begged by the singer to sound only in his sweetheart's ears; from its strumming in the accompaniment and the tuneful entreaty of the lover, Schubert shapes a vivacious little serenade. The second song, composed in June 1827, is 'Das Lied im Grünen'; the poem is by Friedrich Reil. The ripple of the pianoforte suggests that from the poet's many springtime images, the mention of the brook has taken Schubert's fancy. The greeting to spring inspires a series of enchanting tunes, as spontaneous as anything he composed. They form a miniature rondo: the melody of the first verse is in A major, and of the second in D major with a glance at B flat major; then there is a return to the original melody in A major. In the last verse the poet pauses for a moment in his rhapsodic contemplation of the delights of spring; we do not know what lies ahead, he admits. The rippling accompaniment does not cease, but the rhythm of the melody is broken momentarily and the words are sung to a thoughtful little phrase. Then the happiness is reasserted and in the postlude the pianoforte sings, for the last time, springtime! springtime! It is an entrancing codetta to the rondo. Schubert's song was published after his death and the publisher, understandably influenced by its attractive melodies, added two more verses from Reil's poem to the basic four selected by Schubert for his song. This is a pity: one *can* have too much of a good thing and the swift, irresistible glimpse of spring in this song becomes blurred if all six verses are sung.

The form of the first melody has an interesting point of construction, for the final phrase is an exact reversal of the initial one:

EX. 17

This musical pattern is another of Schubert's 'images'; its recurrence can be found in many of his songs to poems dealing with spring.

VIII

SWAN SONG

During October 1827 Schubert spent a holiday at Graz, a town
ideally situated in the Styrian countryside. The poet Karl von
Leitner lived in the district. It is not unlikely that Schubert's
cultured hosts, Karl and Marie Pachler, mentioned him and
his work, but the two men never met. Leitner's name was not
unknown to the composer since he had already, in 1823, set
one of his poems to music. This is 'Drang in die Ferne', the song
of a youth who wants to spread his wings and make his own
way in the world. Notated in 9/8, the music is a Viennese waltz,
full of boisterous gaiety, but capable also of a touch of melan-
choly when the lad's words grow wistful. It is one of those songs
where the left hand does all the work of accompanying, leaving
the right hand free to embellish the voice part with its own
delightful counterpoint. But during and after the visit to Graz
Schubert set seven more Leitner poems. Only 'Die Sterne' equals
the 1823 song in Schubertian charm. To the watching poet the
stars seem to console and to promise good fortune. The
accompaniment transmutes their twinkling into a light, dancing
measure. The song is in E flat major and its charm lies in
Schubert's unexpected moves into related keys, C major, C flat
major and G major, for the varying sentiments in each stanza.
It is an attaching little song.

The two poets Ludwig Rellstab and Heinrich Heine belong
exclusively to Schubert's last year. Each is responsible for a
group of songs having that distinctive tone which marks them
off as a separate entity. There are altogether ten settings of
Rellstab if we include 'Auf dem Strome', the song with horn
obbligato which Schubert composed specially for his concert of
March 1828.[1]

He intended to publish a collection of songs on Rellstab texts
and he began, early in 1828, by setting two poems, 'Lebensmut'
and 'Herbst'. Later in the year he did further work on Rellstab's
poems and completed seven more songs; these are as famous as
the first two are obscure. They were published posthumously as
the first seven of fourteen songs known as *Schwanengesang*.

[1] The indication that the violoncello may be used as an alternative to the
horn is unauthentic, in the sense that it nowhere derives from Schubert.

Schubert's death prevented the execution of his own scheme, for it was far from his intention to have these fourteen songs grouped together; *Schwanengesang* was, in fact, a doubtful venture on the part of his brother Ferdinand and the publisher Tobias Haslinger.

'Lebensmut' (D. 937) was composed in one magnificent flight of exuberant creative fancy. Blood flows like fire in our youth, says the poet; make something of life before the fire dies. The song recalls 'Mut' in *Winterreise* and there is more than a hint of 'Auf dem Wasser zu singen' in the accompaniment. We have only Schubert's first manuscript and it is considered unfinished; a glance at the last bar is sufficient to indicate that it is complete in all but repeat-marks for succeeding verses. Nevertheless, it remains a sketch for it is impracticably high and the composer's fair copy would doubtless have been made in a lower key. 'Herbst' failed to appear in *Schwanengesang* because Schubert wrote it in a friend's album, which was not discovered until the 1890s. It is a song as fine as any of the Rellstab settings. The words are conventional – a remembrance of summer's happiness as the autumnal winds herald winter. Schubert's sombre E minor harmonies and the unceasing sough of the wind in the tremolo accompaniment paint an unforgettable picture.

Apart, possibly, from 'Frühlingssehnsucht' and 'In der Ferne', the Rellstab songs of *Schwanengesang* are all well known and very popular. 'Liebesbotschaft' is the song of a contented lover, who sends greetings to his sweetheart; he confides them to the brook, which is given expression by Schubert's inexhaustible power of inventing pianoforte images to represent flowing water. The threefold melody has grace, warmth and simplicity. 'Kriegers Ahnung' is the last of Schubert's episodic songs; the soldier's presentiment of his death in coming battle is all the more bitter because of his happy love. The scene of the sleeping camp, the dying embers and the lonely silence, is pictured in the music, which is dramatic and full of colour. It contains a Schubertian feature typical of his work in 1828, which can be found also in 'Herbst' and 'Aufenthalt': a jarring juxtaposition of unrelated chords drives home a point in the text. In 'Kriegers Ahnung' the phrase 'ganz allein' ('quite alone') is sung twice; the first time it is illustrated by the association of the chords of F sharp minor and A minor, the second time by the even more extravagant association of A minor and F minor. The interludes, in which the soldier bids farewell to his dearest, are melodious and emphasize the dramatic episodes which enclose them. 'Ständchen', like 'Ave Maria', has been cheapened by its exceeding popularity; it is an entrancing serenade and perhaps after the undeserved shelving it now receives, it will again take its place as one of Schubert's most attractive love-songs. 'Aufenthalt' is another essay in the style of 'Herbst'. The storm and the rocky landscape give Schubert his opportunity; he depicts them in the relentless drive of the pianoforte chords and with this accompaniment as a 'subject' he works his usual harmonic and structural miracles. The voice part is boldly drawn and technically difficult. The last of the Relfstab songs is 'Abschied'. The 'goodbye' is said by a student, riding on his pony and leaving the town for good; 'goodbye' to houses, gardens, the river and – but this is hard! – the girls. It is a captivating song; the trotting of the pony is heard in the staccato quavers of the pianoforte, and the key changes deftly as we ride past the various scenes of the farewells.

The six poems by Heine were chosen by Schubert from the first part of a series of lyrics called *Die Heimkehr*. The title of each song was given by Schubert. It is doubtful if the order in which they appear in *Schwanengesang* is according to Schubert's wish, for it differs considerably from the order in *Die Heimkehr*. Heine's lyrics are partly autobiographical and the sequence, although not narrative, is coherent. The altered order in *Schwanengesang* destroys this coherence and gives us an unconnected group of songs in which 'Das Fischermädchen', for example, seems out of place. It should actually be the first song and as such would introduce us to the woman whom the poet loved and lost.

'Der Atlas' describes the burden of unsatisfied love borne by the poet. It is in Schubert's greatest vein, a trenchant and passionate outcry. The tonal scheme – G minor: B major: G minor – embraces the wide-ranging harmonies on which Schubert calls to convey the poet's heart-break and wounded pride. There is a detail in the musical structure worth considering because of its wider implications; it is an augmented interval associated in the composer's mind with doomed love. We find it in 'Der Zwerg' when the dwarf gazes on the dead queen:

In 'Die junge Nonne' it occurs in connection with the nun's renunciation of love:

Its finest use is in 'Der Atlas':

In this song it is developed on almost symphonic lines.

The poet stands before the portrait of his lost love in 'Ihr Bild'. The extreme economy by which Schubert conveys the loss, the illusion of a smile on the lips of the painted face, and the tears which cause that illusion, is pure genius. The melody is in B flat minor, and modulates into G flat major for the fancied smiling; a return to B flat minor and a Schubertian close in the major embodies the lover's words: 'I cannot believe that I have lost her'. 'Das Fischermädchen' returns to the world of Schubertian lyricism at its happiest and most endearing. From the dancing 6/8 rhythm in the pianoforte part the melody springs and hovers like a bird. It is sung to all three verses, but the modulation from A flat to C flat for the second verse maintains the freshness of its appeal by the simplest means.

The next two songs, 'Die Stadt' and 'Am Meer', are settings of poems with the sea as a very important factor in the conveying of the heavily charged emotions. The most casual glance shows that they were published in the wrong order, an arrangement which has obscured the fact that they actually form a pair of songs. To Schubert, of course, the sea was simply a colourful literary image, but it is doubtful whether he could have depicted it more vividly in these two songs if he had lived by it all his life. It stretches wide, lit by the last rays of the sunset, in 'Am Meer'; the calm, diatonic harmony supports a melody of great beauty, requiring almost superhuman breath control to sustain its long, gracious line. The mist rises, the woman's tears fall, and the music is full of the lovers' heartbreak. In 'Die Stadt' there is a further example of the composer's unequalled power of pictorial representation in the music he designed for the accompaniment. The poet looks towards the distant shore from a rowing-boat and a fitful wind disturbs the grey waters. A series of arpeggios shivers in the accompaniment – an extraordinarily impressive device:

EX. 19

A ray from the sun breaks through and shows him the town where he loved and lost. The arpeggios cease momentarily and in the tragic C minor plaint we share his vision. Then the mists close again.

The last of the Heine songs is the celebrated, the immortal 'Der Doppelgänger'. The midnight loneliness of the streets, and the vision of the spectre which mocks the lover's agony in past years, transported Schubert. The song is far and away his finest use of the blend of declamation and song. How far we have come from Reichardt's 'deklamiert' and 'gesungen'! The words are sung to melodious recitative, flexible enough to serve every demand of the text. At the cry 'Why do you ape my agony?' the music tears its way from B minor to a *fortissimo* in D sharp minor. The closing phrase, subsiding almost to inaudibility as the silence and darkness of the streets reassert themselves, is the most pathetic in Schubert, full of heartache and protest.

In conclusion it may be of interest to give the order of the six songs as they occur in Heine's *Die Heimkehr* and to show how, arranged thus, they do form a miniature song-cycle: 'Das Fischermädchen'; 'Am Meer'; 'Die Stadt'; 'Der Doppelgänger'; 'Ihr Bild'; 'Der Atlas'.

61

The *Schwanengesang* closes with Seidl's 'Die Taubenpost'. There is no suggestion in its cheerful pages of the depths which Schubert had plumbed in the Heine songs. The technical perfection and polished detail, however, reveal the experienced composer in every note. The poem relates the confidences of a happy lover whose thoughts fly to his sweetheart as hers, he knows, fly to him; the carrier-pigeon of the title, who conveys the messages, is 'longing'. In his earlier years Schubert would doubtless have set the poem as a simple, strophic song, but the imagery is now too tempting. The interlinked melodies, coloured by his ever-changing, ever-fresh modulations, are accompanied by a syncopated dance-rhythm which suggests plucked strings. The ejaculated questions and answers of the lover at the end of the song break the melody into fragments, but the steady dance of the pianoforte part binds them all into a harmonious whole. 'Die Taubenpost' will always hold a special place in the affections of the Schubertian, by reason of the fact that it is his last song; but it justifies that esteem by its own charming and amiable qualities.

In the same month, October 1828, Schubert composed 'Der Hirt auf dem Felsen', a solo cantata differentiated from the main body of his *Lieder* by the addition of a clarinet obbligato. The words are drawn for the work of two authors, Wilhelm Müller and Wilhelmina von Chézy (who wrote the play *Rosamunde*). It was composed as a showpiece for the famous operatic singer Anna Milder-Hauptmann and as such exploits the technical possibilities of a powerful soprano voice. The shepherd in the poem longs for the coming of spring – the end of winter and of his loneliness. The lovely, graceful lines of the melody at the start make an immediate appeal, and the greater Schubert is heard in the middle section, with the long-drawn, melodious plaint of the shepherd. The final *allegretto* is buoyant coloratura; voice and clarinet vie in a joyful welcome to the spring.

Within a month of writing this song Schubert died. The last page in the volumes of songs, from 'Gretchen am Spinnrade' to 'Die Taubenpost' was written. So far as he knew, and as his friends believed, their appeal was ephemeral. But from that day onwards those volumes have remained open, and they will never be closed while music endures.

INDEX OF SONGS

Individual songs in *Die schöne Müllerin*, *Schwanengesang* and *Winterreise* are not listed.